jazz PERFORMER
Standards for Advanced Solo Piano

American Treasures

Arranged by Tony Caramia

AF893928

The arrangements in this collection arose from a chance discovery. On the inside front and back cover of a piece of sheet music from 1942, I came across two advertisements. Each promotion was titled "Music for Americans: Four of a series of ten piano compositions by distinguished modern American composers." Below that heading were four-measure music samples of each of the pieces. Their titles all included the word "American," and the pieces were written by a variety of composers. A few of the pieces included "March for Americans" by Ferde Grofé, "American Lullaby" by Duke Ellington, "American Humoresque" by Sigmund Romberg, and "American Barcarolle" by Harry Warren. With the assistance of the Sibley Music Library at the Eastman School of Music, interlibrary loan, and online resources, I was able to locate scores for all of the ten pieces. To my delight, two were still in print—"American Minuet" by Harold Arlen and "American Caprice" by Morton Gould—and the other eight pieces had been arranged by composer, conductor, and publisher Domenico Savino. Originally, the ten pieces had been commissioned by Meredith Willson (later of *The Music Man* fame) for orchestra. Willson had conducted the orchestral versions for a radio program, which he had directed. I realized that four of the pieces lend themselves especially well to the piano and to modern reharmonizations and textures. These are four of the selections contained in this folio. I have also included an arrangement of "America the Beautiful," which I envision almost without tempo—a sort of rumination or meditation on the music. I hope the mixture of old and new material provides pianists and audiences with enjoyment for years to come.

—Tony Caramia

To my dear friend and colleague, Jim Lyke, who helped me discover many American musical treasures.

Alfred

Produced by
Alfred Music Publishing Co., Inc.
P.O. Box 10003
Van Nuys, CA 91410-0003
alfred.com

Printed in USA.

ISBN-10: 0-7390-8376-7
ISBN-13: 978-0-7390-8376-5

Cover Photo
Lattice: © istockphoto / ColinBroug

America the Beautiful

Samuel A. Ward
Arr. Tony Caramia

13
16
sub. p
19
22
Easy swing
molto rit.
25

28
31
34
37
molto rit.
39
Delicately
p
mp
legato
pedal ad lib.

42
move ahead
hold back
a tempo
pp
p
45
cresc.
rit.
48
A little slower
mp dolce
51
mf
poco rit.
54
molto rit.
pp
ppp

American Arabesque

Vernon Duke
Arr. Tony Caramia

12
15
even eighths
poco rit.
18
a tempo
mp
21
mp
24
poco rit.
p

27
Easy swing
mp
mel.
30
even eighths
33
rit.
A little slower, expressively
36
even eighths
39

42
45
48
poco rit.
Easy swing
51
mp
54

57
Push ahead
even eighths
poco rit.
molto rit.
mp
60
63
mp
cresc.
66
f
69

72
pp poco rit.
Easy swing
75
mp
pedal ad lib.
even eighths
78
81
mp
84
swing
f

AMERICAN NOCTURNE

Dana Suesse
Arr. Tony Caramia

14
17
mf
poco rit.
dim.
19
molto rit.
p
Più mosso
21
mp
25
mp

29
mf
32
p
35
mp
38
41

45
mp
48
p
51
mf
pp
54
57
mp
8va

60
start slowly
accel.
8va
molto accel.
Più mosso
61
64

67
69
72
poco rit.
cresc.
poco accel.
pedal ad lib.
76
molto cresc.
poco rit.
molto rit.
ff
fff
79
Slowly and sadly
mf
molto rit.
ppp
8va

American Serenade

Louis Alter
Arr. Tony Caramia

Gently swaying (♩ = 72–80)

13
15
poco accel.
cresc.
18
poco rit.
21
a tempo
mf
23

25
27
29
32
poco rit.
poco cresc.
35
molto rit.

37
Più mosso
39
41
43
rit.
a tempo
mp
46

49
51
mf
54
56
58

60
62
8va
a tempo
rit.
mf
65
8va
sfz
Rather quickly
8va
68
sfz
rit.
Broadly and majestically
71
molto rit.
ff

73
74
76
77
78

80
Tempo I
mf
83
poco cresc.
rit.
Slower, sadder
86
p
LH
89
mp
dim.
91
molto rit.
espress.
p
8va

American Waltz

Peter De Rose
Arr. Tony Caramia

With a gentle sway, in one (𝅗𝅥. = 54–60)

13
a tempo
pp
p
18
poco cresc.
mf
22
4
2–5
dim.
26
4
3
3
30
6
cresc.
6
6
LH

33
p
poco cresc.
mf
38
4–5
f
dim.
43
a tempo
poco rit.
p
47
8va
a tempo
poco rit.
51
mp
pedal ad lib.

55
mf
59
f
63
dim.
mf poco rit.
a tempo
67
f
pedal ad lib.
71
mf

75
f
pedal ad lib.
poco rit.
79
a tempo
8va
mf
83
poco rit.
poco accel.
cresc.
88
poco rit.
accel.
91
a tempo
f
cresc.
pedal ad lib.

95
ff
99
mf
103
molto rit.
107
a tempo
f
cresc.
111
ff

115
poco rit.
119
mp
molto rit.
a tempo
p
123
127
130
pp
ppp